Great People, Great Events

by Barbara Mitchelhill

Contents

Longman

Edinburgh Gate
Harlow, Essex

Samuel Pepys

A long time ago, there was a man called Samuel Pepys.
He lived in London. In 1660, he began to keep a diary.
It was a secret diary. He wrote it in code. Many years
later, the code was broken. Then people could read it.

The diary tells us about Samuel's life. It tells us how he went to Holland on a ship in 1660. King Charles II was staying there. The King had run away from England. He was afraid he would be killed. Samuel met the King and came back with him to London. People were glad.

In 1665, the plague came to London. The summer was hot. The streets were filled with rotting rubbish. Rats were everywhere. The disease spread quickly. Samuel put a hare's foot in his pocket. He thought it would keep him safe from the plague. In his diary, he wrote about the things he saw. He told how sick families were locked in their houses. Red crosses were painted on their doors to show they had the plague. Everyone was afraid. By the end of the year, thousands of people had died.

The next year, there was another disaster in London.
Fire broke out in Pudding Lane. It spread through the city.
Samuel thought his house would burn down. He wanted to
get away. He loaded a cart. Then he and his family left
their home. The fire raged for four days. Samuel wrote
about it in his diary. "I wept when I saw it. Churches and
houses were all on fire."

Three years later, Samuel's wife died. He was very sad. He stopped writing his diary. But Samuel still worked hard. He was a clever man and became an MP. He liked reading and he liked books. He had lots of them in his house. When he died, he left 3000 books. Six of these were his secret diary.

The Great Fire of London

In 1666, a baker lived in Pudding Lane. One night, when he was fast asleep, someone knocked at the door. When the baker woke up he found that his house was on fire.

A spark from the bread oven had started the fire. Smoke was everywhere. The baker and his family climbed out of the bedroom window. Then they went over the roof to the next house.

The fire soon spread down Pudding Lane. Then it went into the next street … and the next. In those days, London streets were narrow. The houses were made of wood. They burned easily. There were no fire engines to help. So people ran for their lives.

They took what they could carry. Many people ran down to the river. They jumped into boats and boatmen took them to the other side of the river.

They thought they would be safe there because fire cannot cross water. But the fire began to spread across London Bridge. People thought it would spread to the other side of the river. But luckily, the flames went out halfway across the bridge.

The sky was black with smoke. Flames were almost at the yards where coal and oil were kept. If the fire kept spreading, London would be destroyed. The King sent soldiers to help. They blew up houses with gunpowder. This made a firebreak.

The fire burned for four days. Then the wind dropped. It began to rain and the fire went out. After that, the ruined houses were cleared away. Better houses were built. These were made of stone and brick. Streets were wider. Many fine churches were built, too. The most famous was St Paul's Cathedral. You can still see it today.

St Paul's Cathedral

13

Mary Seacole

Mary Seacole was born in Jamaica in 1805. Her father was a soldier in the British Army. Her mother ran a boarding house for sick soldiers. Mary learned how to care for them. She learned how to mix medicine. One year, there was a terrible disease. It was called cholera. At first, many people died. But then Mary helped to find a cure.

When Mary was grown-up, she set up boarding houses to look after the sick. Then a war broke out in the Crimea. Britain and other countries sent soldiers to fight there. Mary knew that many soldiers would be hurt. They would need her help.

Britain

The Crimea

Jamaica

So in 1854 Mary set sail for London and went to the War Office. She asked if she could be a nurse in the Crimea. But the men there said no. They said that soldiers would not want a black woman to nurse them.

Mary did not give up. She went to the Crimea and tried to join Florence Nightingale's nurses. But she was turned down. Then she went to the front line where the fighting was. There were many injured soldiers, but there was no hospital. So Mary set up a hospital of her own.

Each day, Mary worked at the hospital. When she had finished, she walked through the battlefield. Guns were firing and she could have been killed. But still she went. She gave medicine to sick soldiers. She bandaged those who were wounded. She stayed with those who were dying. Everyone called her Mother Seacole.

When the war was over, Mary had no money to get back home. The soldiers heard about this and they collected money for her. Soon she was back in London. She was given two medals for bravery. Then she wrote a book about her life and it became a bestseller.

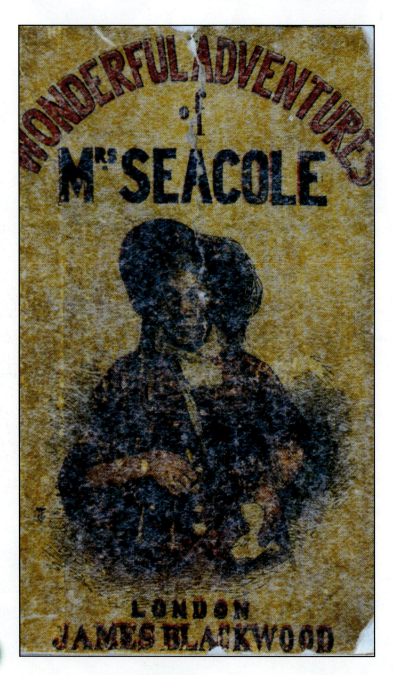

The Coronation of Queen Victoria

Victoria was on her way to Westminster Abbey. It was Thursday morning, 28th June 1838. She was going to be crowned Queen. The guns in the park and the noise of the crowds had woken her up in the night. It seemed that everyone had come to London for this day.

Inside Westminster Abbey, every seat was taken. Some people had been there for hours. When Victoria walked in, everyone turned to look. Slowly, she went to the throne and the coronation began. It lasted for five hours.
A beautiful robe was put round her shoulders and the crown was placed on her head.
Then trumpets sounded. Guns were fired and everyone in the Abbey cheered. She wrote later, "I shall remember this day as the proudest of my life."

As Queen Victoria walked back down the aisle, young ladies-in-waiting carried the train of her dress. This was a great help, because the crown and the robe were very heavy.

The golden coach took Victoria from the Abbey. Crowds of people lined the streets. They had been waiting all day to see her. As the coach came near, they shouted, "God save the Queen!" They cheered and pushed forward.

Victoria wrote in her diary: "I was alarmed at times for fear that the people would be crushed." She also wrote, "How proud I feel to be the Queen of such a nation."

That night there was a grand dinner. But when it was over,
Victoria still had one thing left to do. She raced up the
stairs to her room. She was going to bath her little dog,
Dash. She could not let anything stop her from doing that!
As she bathed him, fireworks lit up the night sky. It was a
perfect end to Victoria's Coronation Day.

Robert the Bruce

About 700 years ago, Scotland was in trouble. King Edward of England had sent his soldiers to fight the Scots. The Scottish King was in prison in London, and Scotland was without a leader. There were many battles with Edward's army. In the end, Edward won. The English King now ruled Scotland.

After that, things got worse. People were turned out of their homes. Their land was taken. Some had to live on the wild hills and some lived in caves like outlaws. One of them was a man called Robert the Bruce. People knew he would make a good leader, so they decided to make him King of Scotland.

More than anything, Robert wanted to defeat the English.
He needed a strong army to fight for Scotland. Men came
to join Robert's army, but they only had swords and axes
to fight with. The English army was bigger and the soldiers
also had bows and arrows. Many Scots died in battle.
Robert's wife and daughter were taken and one of his
brothers was killed.

Robert ran for his life and hid in a cave. He had almost given up hope. Then, one night, he watched a spider on the roof of the cave. It was trying to make a web. At first, the spider fell down. But it did not give up. It tried again and again and again. Robert saw that he should be like the spider and keep on trying.

Watching the spider taught Robert not to give up hope. He decided to go back to his people. Together they would get rid of the English.

Robert gathered a small army again. They marched to
Bannockburn where they met King Edward's army. The
English soldiers thought they would win the battle because
their army was much bigger. But Robert was clever. He
had planned the battle very carefully. This time, they beat
the English. Scotland was free again – thanks to Robert
the Bruce!

Remembrance Sunday

At the beginning of November, you will see people selling poppies. They sell them in shops and in lots of different places. Many people buy a poppy and wear it very proudly. They do it to remember all those who died in wars. The money that comes from selling poppies is used to help people who fought in wars – and the families of those who died.

The First World War started in 1914. Men from Britain and other countries went to fight against Germany. The war lasted for four years and many, many people were killed.

At last everyone agreed to stop fighting. They stopped at eleven o'clock on the eleventh day of the eleventh month. The following year, red poppies began to spring up on the battlefields. Some people said that there was a flower for every person who had died. This is why the poppy is used as a sign of remembrance.

In 1939 the Second World War started. This was an even bigger war than the First World War. It lasted until 1945 and millions of people were killed.

There is a special day for remembering all the people who died in wars. The Sunday nearest to the eleventh day of the eleventh month (11th November) is called Remembrance Sunday. All over Britain there are services of Remembrance. People say prayers and place poppy wreaths on war memorials. At eleven o'clock there is a two-minute silence.

In London there is a big parade which you can see on television. People who were in the army, navy or the air force march past the Cenotaph. The royal family and the prime minister are the first to lay their wreaths of poppies. The Service of Remembrance shows that people who died fighting for their country will not be forgotten.